Positive Alp
Affirmations for Kids

52 Mindful Affirmations to Inspire Positivity, Build Kids Confidence, Self Esteem, Kindness and More.

Written by Leesa McGregor

Positive Alphabet Affirmations for Kids

To download a FREE Children's Empowerment Kit, visit www.AlphabetforHumanity.com/gift

ISBN 978-1-7751413-7-2

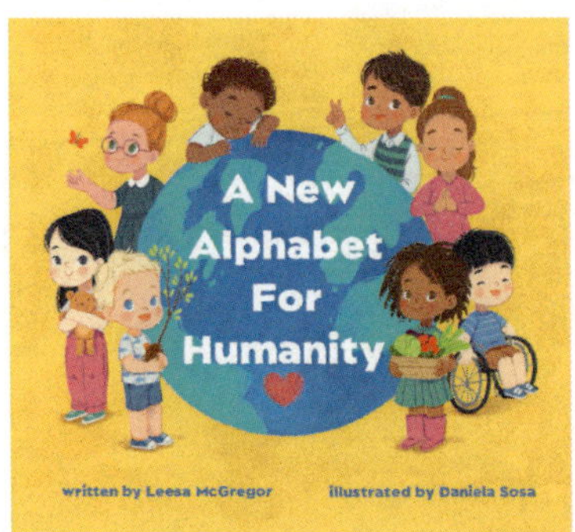

More available:
A New Alphabet for Humanity
A #1 best selling book for raising kind, confident and caring kids.

For more ideas and inspiration, visit: www.AlphabetforHumanity.com

This book belongs to:

Positive Alphabet Affirmations for Kids

Dear Parents and Teachers,

My name is Leesa McGregor. I have dedicated my life's work to making a difference and inspiring positive change.

Two years ago I got inspired to write a best selling book called A New Alphabet for Humanity, to empower children everywhere to be compassionate, kind and loving to people and the planet.

I've always believed that our thoughts have the power to shape our lives. Positive Alphabet Affirmations for Kids is perfect for learning about the power of positivity, and being conscious of our thoughts and words. It's the perfect compliment to A New Alphabet for Humanity!

Inside, you'll discover more than 50 powerful affirmations you can share with children at home or in the classroom to cultivate kindness, empathy, compassion, mindfulness and more.

Early learning lasts a lifetime. The intention behind these affirmations is to help children to cultivate a positive mindset and a strong early foundation for confidence, happiness and success.

To parents and teachers everywhere, thank you for sharing these affirmations with the children in your life.

Together we can change the world.

With Love and Kindness,

Leesa McGregor

A is for Abundance

There is enough for you and enough for me.

A is for Abundance

I am generous. The more I give to others, the more I receive.

B is for Bravery

I am brave. I have the courage to try new things.

B is for Bravery

I believe in myself.
I am capable of anything.

C is for Compassion

I am compassionate. I love to show others how much I care.

C is for Compassion

I have compassion for myself and others. I care about people.

D is for Diversity

I enjoy and appreciate what makes everyone different.

D is for Diversity

I respect people who are different than me. I see the best in everyone.

E is for Empathy

I understand and care about other people's feelings.

E is for Empathy

I am caring and thoughtful.
I am a great listener.

F is for Forgiveness

It is easy for me to forgive and hold love in my heart instead.

F is for Forgiveness

I am forgiving and kind.
I can forgive myself and others.

G is for Gratitude

I am grateful for all the wonderful things in my life.

G is for Gratitude

I am grateful for who I am.
I am grateful for what I have.

H is for Happiness

I am happy. I think cheerful thoughts and have fun everyday.

H is for Happiness

I choose to be happy.
Each day my happiness grows.

I is for Imagination

I am filled with creative ideas.
I have a wonderful imagination.

I is for Imagination

I believe in my dreams.
I can be anything I want to be.

J is for Joyful

I am joyful. I love doing things that make me smile.

J is for Joyful

Today I choose joy. I shine my light wherever I go.

K is for Kind

I act with kindness.
I enjoy helping others.

K is for Kind

I am gentle and caring.
I am thoughtful and kind.

L is for Loving

I love myself just the way I am.

L is for Loving

I am lovable. I am surrounded by love.

M is for Mindful

I take a moment to pause and breathe. I listen to what I need.

M is for Mindful

I am mindful of my thoughts and feelings. I listen to my heart.

N is for Nurturing

I can make a difference.
I can nurture the earth.

N is for Nurturing

I take good care of the world around me.

O is for Optimistic

I always see the bright side.
I find the good in every day.

O is for Optimistic

I am optimistic. I fill my mind with positive thoughts.

P is for Peaceful

Peace in the world begins with peace in my heart.

P is for Peaceful

**I am happy and peaceful.
I let my heart lead the way.**

Q is for Quality

I love spending quality time with others.

Q is for Quality

I make time for happy moments in my day.

R is for Respectful

I am respectful towards others and the earth.

R is for Respectful

I treat people the way
I would like to be treated

S is for Sincere

I speak from my heart and share how I feel.

S is for Sincere

I am honest and sincere.
I am trustworthy.

T is for Thankful

I give thanks for my day and the people I love.

T is for Thankful

I am thankful for all the good things in my life.

U is for Unity

I like working together to make things better.

U is for Unity

I am a peacemaker. I share my love with the world.

V is for Vibrant

I am vibrant.
My body is full of energy

V is for Vibrant

I take good care of my body.
I am healthy and strong.

W is for Wise

I am capable and smart.
I enjoy learning new things.

W is for Wise

I am proud of myself. I love to learn and grow everyday.

X is for Exhale

I take a deep breath.
I feel calm and relaxed.

X is for Exhale

My mind is calm.
I feel peaceful inside.

Y is for Yes

I am open to new ideas.
I enjoy new experiences.

Y is for Yes

**I embrace new challenges.
I can do hard things.**

Z is for Zen

I feel calm and blissful.
I live in the present moment.

Z is for Zen

I let go of my worries.
I feel peaceful and relaxed.

Download Your Free Affirmations Poster and Children's Empowerment Kit (Valued at $27)

To Download Your Free Children's Empowerment Kit, including 5 Printable Posters, Kindness, and Mindfulness Activities, visit: www.AlphabetforHumanity.com

Empowering Children for a Bright Future

Our mission is to help families to raise the next generation of kind, confident and caring kids.

Together, we're leading a movement towards a kinder, more compassionate world.

To receive a FREE Children's Empowerment Kit simply go to: www.AlphabetforHumanity.com

Enjoy The Complete Collection of Alphabet for Humanity Books!

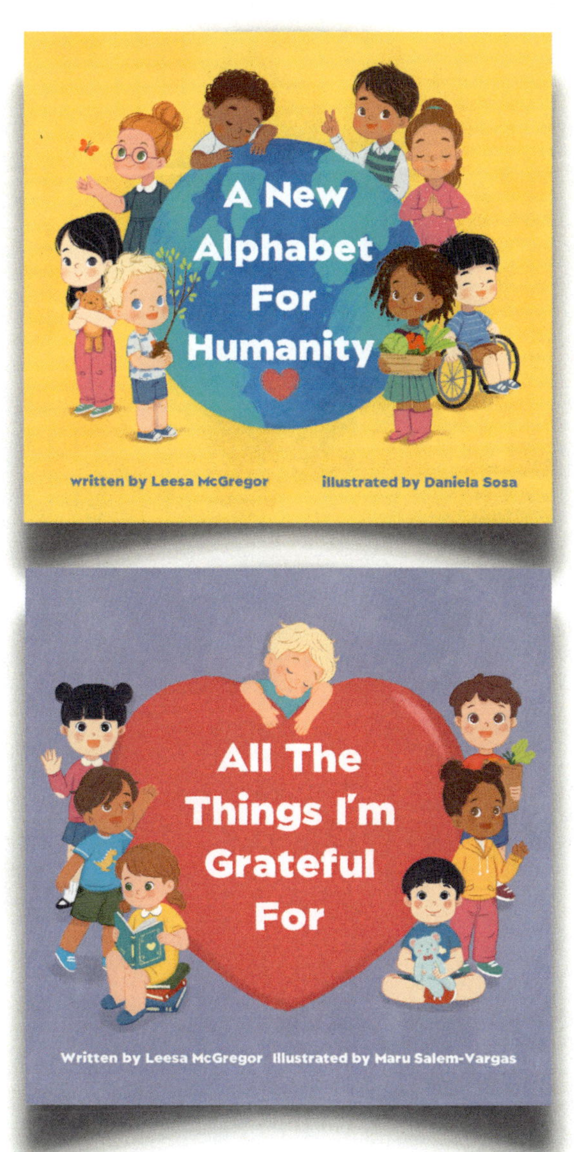

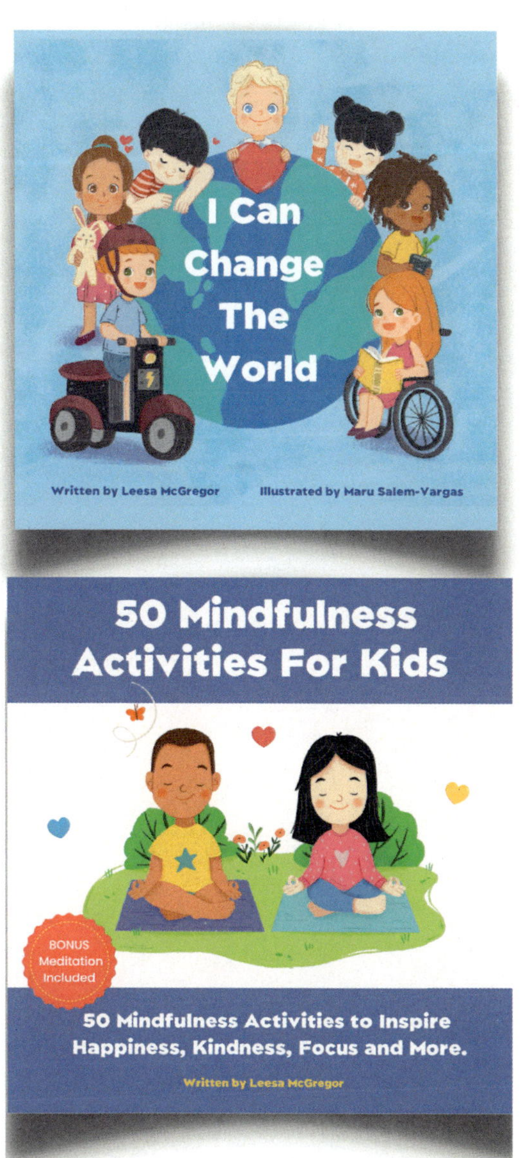

Visit: www.AlphabetforHumanity.com

Made in the USA
Monee, IL
16 July 2022